A Survey of Black Newspapers

by

Henry G. La Brie III

Copyright 1979 by Henry G. La Brie III

International Standard Book Number: 0-89080-034-0

Printed in the United States of America

Note: This survey of black newspapers first appeared in 1970 under the title *The Black Press in America: A Guide*. The information in the *Guide* and in this survey was gathered almost completely through telephone interviews with the publishers and editors. It was hoped by the author that this method would improve upon the accuracy of reporting on the activity of black newspapers. Even so, the circulation figures reported herein are, with the exception of Audit Bureau of Circulations verified papers, impossible to substantiate. The author has encouraged members of the black press and the National Newspaper Publishers Association to move in a direction which would eliminate this condition. Verified circulation figures, either paid or controlled-circulation, would not only enhance the image of these newspapers in their communities and within the media industry but, it is believed, would lend to the permanence of these journals. Unfortunately, since the author began research on this subject in 1969, very little effort has been made to remedy this problem.

ACKNOWLEDGEMENT: Special thanks to *Editor and Publisher*, 575 Lexington Ave., New York, New York 10022 and especially Robert U. Brown, president; Ferdinand Teubner, publisher; and Michael Olver, research director for the support and assistance they provided.

FOREWARD

The idea for this survey dates back to 1970, when the author realized that an accurate, up-dated working list of black newspapers was not available. In fact, the lists of black newspapers supplied by various government agencies and press research groups included mostly journals that were no longer publishing.

An initial effort to ellicit cooperation from the editors and publishers through a mail questionnaire failed when only six of 190 information sheets were returned in March, 1970. Thus, the direct contact which a telephone interview provides was believed to be a step in the right direction. Although a comprehensive basic list was produced in November, 1970, with the assistance of the University of Iowa's Institute for Communication Research, the circulation figures listed were widely (and rightly so) criticized. Later, at a meeting of black publishers and editors, one respected and older publisher complimented the author on his efforts but added that the "circulation figures seemed to have had some yeast added to them."

It has been a primary goal of these surveys to improve upon the quality of information supplied. This most recent analysis reflects significant decreases in both the number of black newspapers publishing and the total circulation. As might be expected, this was met with strong rebuttal from members of the black press. In the May, 1979 issue of **National Scene**, a **Parade**-type supplement produced monthly by L.H. Stanton from his office at 507 Fifth Avenue in New York, Asakia Muhammad in his story "Don't Bury the Black Press Yet" wrote:

> ". . . Henry G. La Brie III proved once again that nothing the Black Press seems to do in the way of journalism seems to satisfy some of its white critics . . ."

Sherman Briscoe, executive director of the National Newspaper Publishers Association in Washington, D.C., wrote in the organization's monthly newsletter of March-April, 1979:

> "Lynching of the black press was attemped in **Editor and Publisher** recently (March 17), in an article by Dr. Henry G. La Brie III, who has been befriended by scores of black publishers. . .Racism still abounds, even among so-called Ph.Ds."

A third rebuttal, appearing on the editorial page of the San Francisco **Sun-Reporter**, was authored on May, 24, 1979 by Thomas Fleming in his column "Weekly Report." In it, he wrote:

> "Dr. La Brie does not appear to recognize or totally ignores the very real fact that television news, as it is presented to the households of the nation, with an overdose of entertainment by the newscasters, poses a serious problem to any vehicle of communication which still uses the printed word as a means of conveying information to the general public. . .He (La Brie) thinks

that the black publishers have sold their souls for advertising gains from white industry, but that accusation could be appropriately made against the entire American press, for one hears the same complaints from some white staff members of the American press about the 'sacred cow' subjects which their editors and publishers will not touch.''

In 1969, when I undertook a research project on the black press which later became my masters thesis at West Virginia University's School of Journalism, I did so with hesitation and misgivings. To begin with, I was white and I wondered then and still do now about the degree of objectivity I might bring to such a study. However, as time moved along, I did in fact receive a great deal of support and assurance from black publishers and editors who were delighted to see that these serious investigations were finally being done. Interviewing almost 75 elderly black journalists, a group I have fondly and respectfully referred to in other articles as Black Pulitzers and Hearsts, was warmly received. The time-consuming and painstaking telephone surveys of the black newspapers provided the most comprehensive working list of black newspapers available anywhere. Time and again, the results of this research won wide acclaim from the members of the black press. And, along the way, I resolved the issue that it is as justified for a white researcher to study black affairs as it is for a black scholar to examine white affairs. However, as in any study, it is critically important to comprehend the depth of understanding and the commitment the researcher has to his subject. Is this a one-time article, without any previous study and without follow-up? Or, is this investigation the results of extensive data gathering and lengthy examination?

A second part of my hesitation and misgiving focused around the fact that I had not even known about the existence of a black press in America, until my advisor, Dr. Guy Stewart, suggested the black press as a possible area for my masters thesis. Here I was at age 22, having been raised in the New York metropolitan area and with an undergraduate journalism degree tucked under my arm and I was totally unaware of not only the black press, but also other minority media. Later still, I was enlightened to discover that we have an active religious press. While this void caused me to hesitate at first, it later became a driving force in my persistance to continue studying the black press, both at the University of Iowa and at Harvard College during my doctoral and post-doctoral periods.

A third reason I initially balked at Dr. Stewart's research proposal was that after a few weeks of library work, it became apparent that the black press had received little if any attention in the major works on journalism in the United States. Further still, the material that was available was often contradictory, superficial and authored by a mass of press researchers, few of whom stopped long enough to contribute a second or third article on the place the black

4

press has had in the American media mix. Notable exceptions to this were Professor Roland Wolseley of Syracuse University and Dr. Armistead S. Pride of Lincoln University. Fortunately, both of these men would later serve as members of my dissertation committee at the University of Iowa and each provided enormous assistance and insight which contributed to the final project results. In short, it seemed to me at first glance, that the black press had been a victim of shoddy analysis. I did not wish to add to this quality and quantity of literature and for that reason, I set what I believed were high standards in research methodology.

I began by seeking out the locations of the black newspapers currently publishing in the U.S. A questionnaire sent by mail failed miserably thus leading to the first telephone survey in 1970 and the publication of **The Black Press in America: A Guide.**

This "personal" contact with the publishers and editors was to a great extent re-assuring. I came to believe that in time, my dedication to accuracy and depth would win over the confidence of most of the interviewees, that the fact that I was white would become a lesser issue than the nature of the study and that eventually, some new ground could be broken in the investigation of this specialized news medium.

There was a definite reluctance on my behalf to write anything critical about the black press. This attitude prevailed for almost five years. I can vividly recall to this day, when the late Dr. Malcolm S. MacLean, Jr., then director of the University of Iowa School of Journalism, called me into his office and asked me how is it that everything I see and write about the black press is good and positive. "Every way of seeing something is a way of not seeing something," he said, and this thoughtful quote lingered with me and in time began to make more sense, not just about the black press but about everything one comes to view.

In retrospect, I believe that I waivered on being critical of the black press in fear that my "sources" and friendships would be jeopardized. Surely, every researcher, every journalist, suffers this agony in one form or another. In fact in the press, we have come to respect shield laws which serve to protect the newspaperman's source.

With the support of the Ford Foundation and the University of Iowa faculty research fund, a core project was completed during the summers of 1971 and 1972. During that time, I interviewed elderly black journalists in 42 U.S. cities in an effort to trace their histories in the black press and better understand why they did what they did. While travelling to collect these taped interviews (now available at Columbia University's Oral History Collection in the Butler Library), I was able to visit 75 black newspaper offices to see first-hand the operations of many prominent black newspapers and some not so well known journals. This was eye-opening and the impressions gathered during these visits helped me to make better sense of Dr. MacLean's comment. Time was also set aside in this project to conduct research on the black press at Atlanta University, Howard University, Morris Brown College, Fisk University, the Library of Congress and the New York Public Library's Schomburg Collection.

Eventually, I began to ask myself what assistance might I be able to lend the black press based upon the research I have accomplished? The first results of this inquiry were reflected in my "Text of Statement" made before members of the Congressional Black Caucus in March, 1972 during hearings held on "The Black Community and the Mass Media." Essentially, I proposed that while the establishment press needs to become more sensitive to reporting accurately the news of the black community, the black community itself needs to become more sensitive about and responsive to the vital role the black press has played and is playing in America today. Rather than being a criticism of the black press, it was meant to be a plea for support from within the black community; and, it strongly advocated expansion of education and training programs which would provide more opportunities for young black students to prepare for a career in the mass media.

Since the testimony made before the Black Caucus, I have intensified my research on the black press in the belief that an accurate assessment of the State of the Black Press might afford the opportunity to advance constructive criticism and new ideas for a black press in transition. It is this analysis which unfortunately seems to have caused many of the publishers and editors conclude that I am predicting the death of the black press; or, the lack of a need for this press. Both feelings are incorrect.

All media go through periods of change. The black press was confronted with its present metamorphosis 25 years ago, when the landmark **Brown vs. the Topeka Board of Education** Supreme Court case beckoned a new era in this country's civil rights movement. The establishment press, which until then almost totally ignored the black community and so-called "black news," was suddenly thrust into covering this critical issue. Gone was the "monopoly" the black press had on the news. And, gone too were many key personnel from black newspapers, who were quickly hired away by good paying establishment media who offered them an opportunity of wide exposure. Here, in fact, is a crisis (even today) for the minority member who considers a career in the media: does he stay with his own press or does he seek employment in the establishment media, harboring the hope and desire to change conditions after he gets "inside." It seems neither answer is correct. Each individual must decide for himself where he feels he can be most helpful.

With their "monopoly" on the news gone and missing many well-trained and respected journalists, the black press began to seek a new direction and place in the media mix of this nation. Limping

6

along at first, struggling to identify new weekly angles on the news which now appeared "daily" in the press, it was, at least through the late Fifties, the most life-threatening period the modern black press (1900-1979) had to face.

It was in the Sixties, with the drama and intensity of a well-organized civil rights movement and a recognition of credibility and faith in black institutions and blackness (and slogans like "Black is beautiful"), that a resurgent black press came to the front and took on again a role of leadership. There were new causes and new battles to be won, perhaps goals which the publishers and editors of the black press in the Forties and Fifties never would have believed attainable.

But, the intensitity of the Sixties gave away to a passivity in the Seventies. A measure of satisfaction over the achievements of the prior decade seemed to temper the tone of the black newspapers. Advertising lineage increased. Now, more and more of the black papers were being conducted as a vocation, a business. For so many years in the past, the editing of a black newspaper had been an avocation rather than a vocation for its publisher.

The consolidation of gains made in the Sixties has ultimately brought about a new crisis for the black press. The cause-oriented newspapers have given way to a medium which appears to be joining other segments of what press researchers refer to as our "community press." As such, these newspapers face new challenges.

No longer will readers buy the paper because it is "owned by a brother." No longer will advertisers take space in an effort to relax organized social and economic pressures. Rather, the black newspaper will be supported based on its ability to report the news, add a new perspective to key issues and supply solutions for the problems which plague the community. More than ever before, black newspapers will today be measured by the tenets of journalism we have come to respect and build upon from Colonial days. Or, in response to Asakia Muhammad's commentary in his **National Scene** article the members of the black press need to work more closely within the parameters of journalism, as we understand them today. Just as we cannot expect the entire automotive industry to adopt the standards established by one make of car, it is absurd to think that the journalism profession embrace the guidelines that have traditionally been associated with many black newspapers.

Thus, what are the specific suggestions that I have been urging publishers and editors to make in order that black newspapers may assume more prominent and permanent positions within the communities they serve? Here are the major ones:

(1) There is and has been a need for some form of cooperative news service focusing on the black community: issues of a national interest; and, problems and solutions which arise in various parts of the country. In a sense, the news service would be a liason for the black press, keeping publishers and editors up-to-date and bringing

the entire black press closer together. It should be remembered that in times of strife, the black press has worked best when it has worked in unity, editorializing nationally about a particular cause.

(2) The National Newspaper Publishers Association, founded in 1940 as the organizational arm of the black press, has several major responsibilities to assume in the final two decades of this century. First, it should plan more intensive professional workshop sessions at its annual convention, a gathering which normally attract about 60 per cent of the nation's publishers and editors. The NNPA members would benefit from learning of new trends, from having their papers critiqued and from developing techniques which would improve the business structure of their enterprises.

Second, the NNPA would do well to creat a "Skills Bank," perhaps at Howard University's School of Communications, where vacancies in the black press can be matched up with candidates interested in beginning their careers. The black press had been and is today short-staffed.

Third, and in conjunction with the second suggestion, the NNPA needs to encourage or lobby for more financial support which would enable a larger group of minority students to matriculate in journalism programs. Also, schools of journalism themselves, need to be individually approached by the NNPA or by black publishers in their respective communities to explore the degree of interest and promotion each school has put into the recruitment of minority students. What course offerings might be added to the curriculum to make the education of minority student journalists more meaningful?

(3) There is a need for more in-depth investigative reporting in the black press. In the past, this characteristic brought significant notoriety and respect to certain of the black newspapers. This type of reporting and follow-up articles related to the subject could not only booster circulation but also make a more definable place for the black press in the media community.

(4) A survey of 75 prominent black journalists, many of them publishers or editors, conducted in 1971, revealed that they placed the editorial page fourth in importance behind society news, sports, and the front page. There is an urgent need to upgrade the position of the editorial page, in the eyes of the publishers and editors as well as their audiences. The editorial page is the launching pad for solutions to community problems; it is the battleground where editors can debate and criticize; and it is the influencing factor that can help to bring about change.

(5) Less than a half dozen black columnists appear weekly in the black press. This critical void of nationally-distributed columnists only serves to compound the problem already existing on the editoral page. The black press would benefit from the emergence of several well-written columns focusing on national and international issues as they affect black affairs.

8

(6) More attention might be paid to the entire typographical make-up of the black newspaper. Layout, use of art, use of white space, photography, headlines, eye-catching layouts; all these deserve more attention. What has been done to train personnel in these areas? Has the editor or publisher made an effort to enroll a staff member in a workshop or college course? Years ago, a press critic referred to the **Norfolk Journal and Guide** as the **New York Times** of the black press. The appearance of a newspaper does in fact promote that newspaper. The National Newspaper Publishers Association sponsors an annual awards contest for the black press and it might be worthwhile to supply members with the specific reasons why the winners won. Perhaps, a follow-up workshop the morning after the awards banquet might attract NNPA members to better understand trends and new techniques. Afterall, the black newspaper has always been a supplement to rather than a substitute for the establishment press. Most households that read a black newspaper probably read an establishment newspaper and it simply makes good sense to have the newsapaer which arrives once a week be able to compete favorably with the daily press in terms of readability.

(7) As a business enterprise, the black newspaper needs to become more assertive in the community. Gone are the days when people will patronage these papers, almost in a charitable fashion, because they are "owned by a brother." And, gone are the days that advertisers will buy space in a black journal solely to appease a segment of the community. Double-digit inflation, swelling inventories, rising interest rates and the threat of a recession have all cautioned the corporate advertiser to inspect readership surveys and request audited circulations. Presently, only 21 black newspapers have verified paid circulations under the comprehensive program monitored by the Audit Bureau of Circulations.

Becoming more "assertive" in the community means the black publisher must continue to re-invest in his business. The paper needs to reflect good management and solvency. This has not been the case at many black newspapers and considering the state some of these offices have fallen into, it is no wonder that these newspapers eventually failed. It would be hard to accept the fact that a newspaper collapses not because it is unable to interpret the events of the day but because the publisher was lax in his business ways.

There are particular "trappings" of the newspaper business and it would do well for members of the black press to identify these, employ these and abide by them in every way possible. Certainly, many of these qualities exist in forms of business: having rate cards readily available; having a skillful receptionist to handle all incoming calls and callers; meeting deadlines; maintaining equipment etc. What might be the peculiar or distinctive guidelines for operating a black newspaper?   **Henry G. La Brie III**
October 16, 1979

9

The Black Press: A Measure of How Far We Have Come

On March 16, 1827, New Yorkers Rev. Samuel Cornish and John Brown Russwurm issued the first black newspaper in America. It was called **Freedom's Journal.**

The editorial in that first edition of the paper provided the **raison d'etre** for a black press: "...We wish to plead our own cause. Too long have others spoken for us. Too long has the public been deceived by misrepresentations in things which concern us dearly..."

Publishing a black newspaper in a white world was a daring thing to do in 1827. With the black population in the United States nearing 2.5 million, almost 60 per cent of this number were living in southern states and Washington, D.C. under a bond of servitude.

However, the State of New York had emancipated many of its slaves by statue in 1827. And, by 1830, slavery in the North had been virtually abolished by legislative or legal action. The North then would be the "birthplace" of the black press.

The first growth period of the black press extended until 1865, with all but one of the estimated 50 newspapers publishing in the North. The loudest voices of the period belonged to Frederick Douglass and Martin R. Delany. Douglass, a runaway slave, was a recognized leader in the abolition movement and to further his cause started **North Star** in Rochester, N.Y. in 1843. Later that same year, Delany, the first black graduate of Harvard University, founded **The Mystery** in Pittsburgh. Considered by many to be one of the earliest black nationalists, Delany wrote: "...The weight of a nation grinds us in the dust...There appears to be a fixed determination on the part of our oppressors in this country, to destroy every vestige of self-respect, self-possession and manly independence left in the colored people..."

It is upon this philosophy of self-determination that the black press survived the first 40 years. The editors of these papers aimed at reaching and appealing to influential white readers. Literacy studies which have been done disclose that one of 20 blacks could read in 1865; one of two could read by 1900.

After the Civil War, black papers appeared in most large cities. Between 1865 and 1900, the second growth period, more than 1,200 black papers were started, 70 per cent in the South.

The black publisher and editor assumed an important role in his community alongside the minister. In most cases, he was a journalist by avocation rather than vocation and the money he made from his regular job along with what little he collected from sales, kept the paper going. Advertising was unheard of.

Historians of journalism have, until recently, neglected to mention the presence of a black press in their writings. Yet, black Pulitzers and Hearsts came on the scene and crusaded for equal opportunity: T. Thomas Fortune and his New York **Age;** Ida B. Wells and her Memphis **Free Speech;** William Monroe Trotter and his

Boston **Guardian;** William Calvin Chase and his Washington **Bee;** Phillip A. Bell and his San Francisco **Elevator;** Chris Perry and his **Philadelphia Tribune;** and John H. Murphy Sr. and his Baltimore **Afro-American.**

Although few of the editors and reporters were able to call upon formal journalism education or previous newspaper experience, they managed to pattern their new coverage around the needs of audiences. The content was wide ranging and a single issue might include short stories, poetry (where else could creative writing by blacks appear?), marriage and birth announcements, sports, editorials and social news.

Lacking business acumen and advertising revenue, many of the newspapers were short lived. In 1950, press scholar Dr. Armistead Pride of Lincoln University estimated that the average lifespan of a black newspaper was nine years.

In spite of being short-staffed, underfunded and untrained, the black press gained significant support and respect in the black community. Combining the tactics of crusading and yellow journalism, the black publisher recognized that he could solidify his position if he could obtain a mass circulation. Afterall, he had a monopoly on "the news."

Out of the South came the leaders of the third growth period: 1901-1970. From Georgia, Robert S. Abbott; from North Carolina, Robert Lee Vann; the Scott Brothers in Atlanta, Ga.; and the Young family in Norfolk, Virginia; all would gain national prominence.

Abbott launched the Chicago **Defender** on May 5, 1905. He sold it on the streets for five cents. Within 15 years, the **Defender** was circulating over 200,000 copies a week nationally. It was the **Defender** that advocated a northern migration and thousands of blacks left the South to settle in Chicago or to work for Henry Ford in Detroit.

Vann came to Pittsburgh to become a lawyer. His interest in poetry brought him into contact in 1910 with five men who had the idea to start a newspaper. Vann offered legal assistance and within a year became a part owner of the **Pittsburgh Courier.** By 1945, the **Courier** would have a national circulation exceeding 300,000.

In Atlanta, William A. Scott started the Atlanta **World** in 1928. Four years later and with help from his brother Cornelius, Scott's paper appeared everyday: the Atlanta **Daily World** was the first successful black daily.

The Norfolk **Journal and Guide** was started in 1909 by P. Bernard Young Sr. Emphasizing accuracy and avoiding sensationalism, the **Journal and Guide** achieved national circulation and respect for being a high quality newspaper.

With circulation revenue increasing after 1920, advertising began to appear. The earliest ads were for skin bleachers and hair straighteners. Big business ignored the black press unaware of the buying power of the black consumer.

After World War II, national advertising began to grow. The civil rights movement picked up momentum and the black press found itself in the thick of campaigns for equality in the armed forces (1948) and in educational opportunities (1954: Brown vs. the Board of Education).

Many press critics claimed that the black press was about to crusade itself right out of business. Rosa Parks boarded the Cleveland Avenue bus in Montgomery, Ala. on December 1, 1955 and decided to sit in the front. It led to her arrest, boycotts, sit-ins and the rise to fame of the pastor at the Dexter Avenue Baptist Church: Dr. Martin Luther King, Jr. The establishment press scrambled to cover the stories and along the way hired reporters from the black press to gather the news.

For the first time, the black press had competition, not only for "the news" but for staff members. The competition has not subsided in the Seventies and the black press has been forced to reconsider its role and the position it should assume in the American media mix. What will the future be?

Over 1,500 black newspapers were started during the third growth period. Today, 165 continue to publish with an average weekly circulation of just over 2.9 million. Only five of these papers have histories which can be traced to before 1900.

The day of the "nationally" distributed black weekly is gone. Today, the black publisher is locally active in identifying community problems and attempting to pose solutions for them. He sees his newspaper as a "supplement to" rather than a "substitute for" the establishment media. He continues to chase national advertising accounts in spite of the fact that economic studies reveal that black America now has buying power exceeding $70 billion.

The black press is no longer a guiding light for millions of Americans. It has become a member of this country's community press. The future of the black press is predicated on its ability to provide another way of looking at some events as well as its ability to be the "sole" reporter of other events which escape the attention of the establishment press. In retrospect, the black press is doing today what it set out to do in 1827, only it is doing it differently. How far we have come in these United States since 1827 might be measured best by the contents of all those papers.

SURVEY ANALYSIS:

A decline in Circulation and Number of Newspapers

As of January 1, 1979, there were 165 black newspapers publishing in 34 states and the District of Columbia. Of this number, 151 reported their circulations which totaled to 2,901,162 weekly.

Compared to a similar survey completed in January, 1974, this represents sharp drops in both circulation and number of papers active. The 1974 study disclosed 213 black newspapers with a total weekly circulation of 4,369,858 (205 papers reporting).

The current survey reflects a 33.6 per cent decrease in circulation and a 22.5 per cent loss in membership papers.

Where is the black press?

Five states contain almost 40 per cent of the black press. Florida, with 17 newspapers, has the largest group of black journals with the most prominent being the **Miami Times** (founded in 1923) and the Tampa **Sentinel-Bulletin** (founded in 1945). The four other states with significant black press activity include California (14 newspapers), Texas (13), New York (12) and Illinois (8).

Employment Statistics:

With 152 papers reporting, it was discovered that 1,880 employees have full-time positions with the black press. Most of these jobs are in the editorial side of the business, since fewer than a dozen black newspapers actually have their own printing facilities.

The 1974 survey reported 2,465 employees which amounts to a 24 per cent decrease in the work force over the five-year period. However, in January, 1974, there were 39 black newspapers with their own printing facilities. This shift toward job printing of the newspaper accounts for the significant difference in the employment figures. Some of the prominent black journals which ceased printing operations include: **Muhammad Speaks** in Chicago (now called the Bilalian News), the **Chicago Daily Defender** and the Norfolk **Journal and Guide.**

Heritage: Not many old papers left

The black press today is a relatively "young" press considering 76 of the newspapers have founding dates after 1960. And, 39 of the papers have been started since 1970.

One of the problems the black newspaper has faced is legacy, and when the publisher has died, often the newspaper has died with him. Fortunately, in many cases, the widow has assumed ownership and control. Some recent examples include: **Mobile** (Ala.) **Beacon;** Houston **Forward Times; Los Angeles Sentinel** and **Minneapolis Spokesman and Recorder.**

Only five of the newspapers have founding dates prior to 1900. This group includes: **Philadelphia Tribune** (1885); **Houston Informer** (1892); Baltimore **Afro-American** (1892); Des Moines **New Iowa Bystander** (1894); and, **Indianapolis Recorder** (1895). These five papers are all "commercial" newspapers. There are three "religious" black newspapers which have pre-1900 births. The three newspapers are: Nashville **Christian Recorder** (1846); Charlotte **Star of Zion** (1876); and Louisville **The American Baptist** (1880).

Methods of Circulation: Four Types

The battle today over the advertising dollar continues to intensify. Newspapers have traditionally competed for advertising lineage and increased their ad rates by being able to prove to the business community that they had growing audited circulations. More recently, newspapers have been forced into backing up their circulation figures with in-depth marketing surveys which provide the advertiser with pertinent information about the audience and areas the papers serve. Sadly, the black press has, for the most part, failed to professionally improve itself in these areas.

In January, 1979, only 21 black newspapers were monitored by the Audit Bureau of Circulations (ABC) and their combined weekly circulations total 435,557. This figure represents only 15 per cent of the entire circulation reported by 151 black newspapers in January, 1979. In other words, 85 per cent of the black press circulation cannot be verified.

Many of the newspapers began an application process with Verified Audit Circulation in Santa Monica, California in 1978. Black Media, Inc., a national advertising representative for many black newspapers (offices in New York City), encouraged its member (estimated at 100) papers to obtain VAC reports. VAC differs from ABC in that it will examine non-paid (controlled-circulation) newspapers and 20 of the black newspapers are currently distributing their issues in this fashion.

The 20 controlled-circulation newspapers represent the second and largest group of black newspapers. Their total weekly distribution figures amount to 942,764 with the Los Angeles **Central News-Wave** (240,455) being the leader.

The third group of black newspapers are those with "publisher's statement paid." These 64 journals have a combined weekly circulation of 868,741 with the leaders being: Nation of Islam's **Bilalian News** (150,000); New York's **Amsterdam News** (83,000); and the Baton Rouge, Louisiana **Community Leader** group of five regional papers (41,400).

The fourth group includes 36 newspapers which have "publisher's statement paid and free" circulations. It was impossible to exactly categorize how each of these newspapers had divided their total circulation since the publishers, editors and staff members interviewed most often did not know what percentage of the distribution was "paid" and what percentage was "free." These 36 papers reported a combined weekly circulation of 654,100. The leaders in this group included: Washington, D.C. **Informer** (55,000); St. Louis **Metro-Sentinel** (36,000); and the **Atlanta Voice** (35,000).

For reporting purposes, the three black daily newspapers listed in Section I and the six bi-weekly newspapers in Section III were not included in the above circulation analysis.

Black Newspapers No Longer Publishing

Since the January, 1974 survey was completed, 24 new listings have been included in the current study. However, 67 newspapers listed in January, 1974 have ceased publication. They have been added to the "No Longer Publishing" section in the rear of the survey. This section should prove to be a handy reference for researchers who may be wondering whether a particular newspaper, not listed in this guide, may still be publishing and therefore may have been overlooked.

Black Newspapers: Advertising Vehicle?

The landmark contributions of the late D. Parke Gibson, the success of **Black Enterprise** magazine and the increasing corporate awareness of the buying power of Black America have collectively contributed to create a very real challenge for the business community: how does one reach this segment of the market.

Surveys which have been conducted within the black community to determine readership habits and the characteristics of information gathering which prevail, indicate overwhelmingly that television is the most persuasive mode of communication. Certainly, many more homes have televisions than subscribe to newspapers. And, within those households which receive newspapers, the black newspaper has always been viewed as a supplement rather than a substitute for the daily newspaper.

Just how aggressively should businesses be in seeking ad space in black newspapers? From the beginning, many businesses have, inpart, owed their growth and success to patronage by the black community. However, it wasn't until after 1945 that some of these corporations recognized this support and began advertising in black newspapers and magazines. During the period 1945-55, black newspapers had a monopoly on the news they reported and because of this fact, they were faithfully read within the community. Businesses owed it to the black press to advertise in these pages, and in return for their support of the black press, (as well as their implementing affirmative action hiring practices), particular corporations were recognized and praised for their foresight.

Today, it is apparent that corporations are, for pragmatic reasons nurtured by the current economic climate, less apt to construct their advertising budgets around concepts of social responsibility. Today, perhaps more than ever before, advertising is being pressured to prove its worth.

Under these conditions and constraints, the black newspaper becomes a wise choice in an advertising program **only** when it can clearly prove to the advertiser that it is a successful enterprise. Afterall, businesses do business best with other successful businesses. What can a black newspaper say to a prospective advertiser about: **1)** verified circulation? **2)** marketing analysis of its subscribers? **3)** demographic survey of the community? **4)** the training of its personnel? **5)** the creativity and enthusiasm of its circulation manager? **6)** the history of the newspaper? **7)** readership surveys the newspaper has contracted?

After a decade of research in this area, it is disappointing to conclude that few black newspapers have taken the time to prove their vitality as an advertising medium. Racism will no longer attract advertising. Businesses would actually strengthen the condition of the black press if they would demand more in the way of evidence which reflects the sophistication of these newspapers. This won't be easy and undoubtedly will cause the demise of some of these newspapers. But, in the end the survivors will be the foundation for an important growth period of this specialized news medium.

I. DAILY BLACK NEWSPAPERS

GEORGIA

Atlanta **Atlanta Daily World**
145 Auburn Ave. N.E. (30303)
(404) 659-1110
22,500 (publisher's statement paid)
Scott Newspaper Syndicate
C.A. Scott
offset
standard
Tuesday, Thursday, Friday, Sunday
1928
35
$5.00/col. inch (national)

ILLINOIS

Chicago **Chicago Daily Defender**
2400 S. Michigan Ave. (60616)
(312) 225-2400
25,000 daily; 25,000 weekend (ABC)
John H. Sengstacke
John H. Sengstacke
offset
tabloid (Monday-Thursday); standard (weekend edition)
Monday-Thursday and weekend edition
1905
75
$.65/line daily; $.70/line weekend edition

NEW YORK

Brooklyn **New York Daily Challenge**
1368 Fulton St. (11216)
sales office: No. 1 Penn Plaza New York City, N.Y.
(212) 760-5555
72,000 (publisher's statement paid)
Thomas H. Watkins Jr.
Thomas H. Watkins Jr.
offset
tabloid
Monday-Saturday
1972
15

II. WEEKLY BLACK NEWSPAPERS

ALABAMA

Birmingham **Baptist Leader**
1417 4th Ave. N. (35203)
(205) 252-6641
4,000 (publisher's statement paid)
Alabama Baptist Publishing Board
W.H. Radney
letterpress
standard
Thursday
1912
4
no advertising

Birmingham **Birmingham World**
312 N. 17th St. (35203)
(205) 251-6523
9,000 (publisher's statement paid)
Scott Newspaper Syndicate
Marcel Hopson
offset
standard
Friday
1932
4
NA

Birmingham **Times**
115 3rd Ave. W. (35204)
    mailing address: P.O. Box 10503 (35204)
(205) 251-5158
36,000 (controlled circulation)
James Lewis
John Streeter
offset
standard
Thursday
1964
14
$5.15/col. inch national; $4.20/col. inch local

Mobile **Inner City News**
(205) 473-2767
Charles W. Porter

Mobile **Mobile Beacon and Alabama Citizen**
2311 Coastarides (36617)
    mailing address: P.O. Box 1407 (36601)
(205) 479-0629
7,000 (publisher's statement paid)
Mrs. L.M. Thomas
Mrs. L.M. Thomas
offset
tabloid
Wednesday
1954
10
$2.10/col. inch (local & national)

Montgomery **Times**
211 Dexter Ave. (36104)
    mailing address: P.O. Box 9133 (36108)
NA
Al Dixon
Al Dixon
offset
standard
Thursday
1977
13
$4.40/col. inch (national)

ARIZONA

Phoenix **Arizona Informant**
222 North 9th Street (85006)
(602) 257-9300
10,000 (publisher's statement paid and free)
Arizona Informant Publishing Co.
Debbie Ellison
offset
tabloid
Wednesday
1971
7
NA

Compton **Metropolitan Gazette**
911 E. Rosecrans (90221)
(213) 635-1471 or 774-0347
61,000 (controlled circulation)
Hillard Hamm
Hillard Hamm
offset
standard
Thursday
1966
11
$.62/line (national)

E. Palo Alto **Peninsula Bulletin**
2332 University Ave. (94303)
(415) 322-6617
9,000 (publisher's statement paid and free)
Charles Thrower
Charles Thrower
offset
tabloid
Thursday
1966
3
$4.38/col. inch (national)

Fresno **California Advocate**
450 Fresno Street (93706)
    mailing address: P.O. Box 3327 (93766)
(209) 268-0941
12,500 (publisher's statement paid and free)
Les Kimber
Mrs. Les Kimber
offset
standard
Wednesday
1967
6
$.24/line national; $2.50/col. inch local

Los Angeles **Central News-Wave** Publications
1016 W. Vernon Ave. (90037)
(213) 232-6221
240,455 -- Group of 8 controlled circulation
  newspapers including:
  Central News (14,850) founded 1953
  Southwest News (44,335) founded 1953
  Southwestern Sun (30,025) founded 1948
  Southwest Wave (65,250) founded 1921
  Southeast Wave-Star (21,765) founded 1938
  Southwest Topics-Wave (27,215) founded 1922
  Southside Journal (30,115) founded 1938
  Englewood Wave (7,000) founded 1972
Chester L. Washington
Chester L. Washington
letterpress
standard
Thursday
Incorporated in 1971
80
$13.58/col. inch for group (national); 2.95/col. inch
  for first paper plus $.90 for each additional paper (local)

Los Angeles **Herald-Dispatch**
374 Stocker (90007)
(213) 295-6323
NA
NA
letterpress
standard
Thursday
1952
17
$.40/line (national and local)

Los Angeles **Los Angeles News**
Manchester Rd. (90047)
(213) 778-0657
15,000 (publisher's statement paid and free) ˙
Reginald Carter
Reginald Carter
offset
tabloid
Sunday
1959
7
$3.00 /col. inch (national and local)

Los Angeles **Los Angeles Sentinel**
1112 E. 43rd St. (90011)
(213) 232-3261
34,000 (ABC)
Mrs. Ruth Washington
James H. Cleaver and Brad Pye Jr.
offset
standard
Thursday
1934
38
$8.40/col. inch national; $3.75/col. inch local

Oakland **California Voice Weekender**
814 27th St. (94607)
(415) 839-9212
29,000 (publisher's statement paid and free)
Dr. Carlton Goodlett
John C. Bailey
offset
standard
Saturday
1919
$2.52/col. inch (national)

Oakland **Post**
630 20th St. (94612)
(415) 763-1120
80,500 -- Group of 5 controlled circulation
          newspapers including:
              Berkeley Post (15,000)
              Oakland Post (54,000)
              Richmond Post (10,000)
              San Francisco Post (15,000)
              Seaside Post (6,500)
Tom Berkley
Tom Berkley
standard
Sunday, Tuesday, Friday
1963
75
$1.80/line national; $11.50/col. inch local (all 5 papers)

Sacramento **Sacramento Observer**
3540 4th Ave. (95801)
   mailing address: P.O. Box 209 (95801)
(916) 452-4781
39,500 (publisher's statement paid)
William H. Lee
William H. Lee
offset
tabloid
Thursday
1962
20
$.64/line national; $5.20/col. inch local

San Bernardino **Precinct Reporter**
1673 W. Baseline (92411)
(714) 889-6808
30,000 (publisher's statement paid and free)
Art Townsend
Stanley Osborne
offset
standard
Thursday
1965
8
$4.25/col. inch (national)

San Diego **Voice and Viewpoint News**
4684 Federal Blvd. (92102)
   mailing address: P.O. Box 95 (92112)
(714) 263-3171
18,000 (publisher's statement paid and free)
Earl Davis, Jr.
Earl Davis, Jr.
offset
standard
Wednesday
1959
11
$4.62/col. inch (national)

San Francisco **Metro**
1366 Turk St. (94115)
(415) 931-5778
82,000 -- Group of 7 controlled circulation
        newspapers including:
        Berkeley Metro Reporter (8,590)
        Oakland Metro Reporter (22,540)
        Peninsula Metro Reporter (12,490)
        Richmond Metro Reporter (9,540)
        San Francisco Metro Reporter (14,480)
        San Jaquin Metro Reporter (7,240)
        Vallejo Metro Reporter (4,440)
Dr. Carlton Goodlett
Don Young
offset
standard
Monday
same staff as **Sun-Reporter**
$1.81/line national; $1.25/line local

San Francisco **Sun-Reporter**
1366 Turk St. (94115)
(415) 931-4081
9,419 (ABC)
Dr. Carlton Goodlett
Thomas Fleming
offset
tabloid
Thursday
1944
23
5
$3.80/col. inch (national & local)

COLORADO

Denver **Denver Weekly News**
2547 Welton St.
(303) 623-6267
10,000 (controlled circulation)
Raymond Hawkins
Stan Swanson
offset
tabloid
Thursday
1971
6
$3.50/col. inch (national)

CONNECTICUT

Hartford **Inquirer**
1023 Albany Ave.
   mailing address: P.O. Box 538 (06101)
(203) 522-1462
68,000 -- A group of four controlled-
        circulation newspapers:
        Hartford (25,000), New Haven (15,000)
        Waterbury (10,000), Bridgeport (18,000)
William R. Hales
William R. Hales
offset
tabloid
Wednesday
1975
10
$6.00/col. inch national; $4.00/col. inch local

DELAWARE

Wilmington **Defender**
1400 French St. (19801)
   mailing address: P.O. Box 1763 (19899)
(302) 656-3252
20,000 (publisher's statement paid and free)
Defender Publishing Co.
Miss A.G. Hibbert
offset
tabloid
Tuesday
1962
8
NA

DISTRICT OF COLUMBIA

Washington **Afro-American**
2002 11th St. N.W. (20001)
(202) 332-0080
6,000 (Tuesday); 7,000 (Friday) - (ABC)
Art Carter
Miss Ruth Jenkins
letterpress and offset
standard
Tuesday (letterpress) and Friday (offset)
1932
25
$.64/line national; $.34/line local

Washington **Capital Spotlight**
2001 Benning, N.E. (20002)
(202) 399-2739 or 399-2771
NA - controlled circulation
R.E. "Ike" Kendrick
R.E. "Ike" Kendrick
letterpress
tabloid
Thursday
1953
5
NA

Washington **Informer**
715 G St. N.W. (20001)
(202) 628-8338
55,000 (publisher's statement paid and free)
Calvin Rolark
Calvin Rolark
offset
tabloid
Thursday
1964
9
$.65/line national; $.35/line local

Washington **New Observer**
811 Florida Ave. N.W. (20001)
(202) 232-3060
25,000 (controlled circulation)
J. Hugo Warren Sr.
J. Hugo Warren Jr.
offset
tabloid
Thursday
1960
9
$.75/line (national and local)

FLORIDA

Daytona Beach **Times**
429 South Campbell St. (32014)
(904) 253-0321
Charles Cherry II

Ft. Lauderdale **Westside Gazette**
1556 N.W. Sistrunk Blvd. (33301)
    mailing address: P.O. Box 9281 (33301)
(305) 584-8760
1.7,000 (publisher's statement paid and free)
Levi Henry Jr.
Levi Henry Jr.
offset
tabloid
Thursday
1971
5
$2.00/col. inch local; $3.24/col. inch national

Ft. Pierce **Chronicle**
1527 Avenue D (33450)
4,000 (publisher's statement paid)
C.E. Bolen
C.E. Bolen
offset
tabloid
Thursday
1957
8
$1.85/col. inch national; $1.40/col. inch local

Jacksonville **Advocate**
410 Broad Street (32206)
(904) 356-0090
Isaiah J. Williams II

Jacksonville **Florida Star-News**
2323 Moncrief Rd. (32209)
    mailing address: P.O. Box 599 (32201)
(904) 354-8880
10,000 (publisher's statement paid and free)
Eric. O. Simpson
Eric O. Simpson
offset
standard
Thursday
1951
12
$3.00/col. inch (national and local)

Miami **Florida Courier**
35 N.E. 17th St. (33132)
(305) 371-3458
10,000 (publisher's statement paid)
John Sengstacke
William Alexander
offset
standard
Saturday
NA
NA
$.30/line (open rate)

Miami **The Liberty News**
Northside Shopping Center Arcade (33147)
(305) 696-8541
C. Gaylord Rolle

Miami **Miami Times**
6530 N.W. 15th Ave. (33147)
    mailing address: P.O. Drawer 47,000 Z, Northwest Branch (33147)
(305) 691-0421
22,014 (ABC)
Garth Reeves
Garth Reeves
offset
tabloid
Thursday
1923
16
$.50/line (national & local)

Orlando **Florida Sun and Mirror**
    mailing address: P.O. Box 2488 (32802)
(305) 838-1912
5,000 (publisher's statement paid)
J. Lawrence Bowden
J. Lawrence Bowden
offset
standard
Thursday
1932
6
$2.50/col. inch national; $2.00/col. inch local

Orlando **Times**
2393 West Church St.
P.O. Box 5339
(305) 298-0660
Pamela Saunders

Pensacola **Pensacola Voice**
213 E. Yonge St. (32503)
(904) 432-5467
8,000 (publisher's statement paid)
Les Humphrey
Les Humphrey
offset
tabloid
Thursday
1971
7
$2.50/col. inch (national)

Riveria Beach **Gold Coast Star News**
1533 W. Blue Heron Blvd. (33404)
(305) 845-0234
5,000 (publisher's statement paid)
Hinton L. Johnson
Hinton L. Johnson
offset
tabloid
Thursday
1971
5
$1.65/col. inch (national and local)

Sarasota **Weekly Bulletin**
2741 N. Osprey Ave. (33578)
   mailing address: P.O. Box 1560 (33578)
(813) 355-6220
15,000 (publisher's statement paid and free)
William F. Jackson
William F. Jackson
offset
standard
Thursday
1959
5
$2.00/col. inch (national & local)

St. Petersburg **Weekly Challenger**
2500 9th St. S. Suite S (33705)
(813) 896-2922
   Tampa Office: 2118 Main St.
                    (813) 251-4368
                    Managing editor-William Blackshear
33,000 (publisher's statement paid and free)
Cleveland Johnson Jr.
William Blackshear
offset
standard
Thursday
1967
8
$4.50/col. inch national; $3.00/col. inch local

Tampa **Sentinel-Bulletin**
2207 21st Ave. (33601)
   Mailing address: P.O. Box 3363 (33601)
(813) 248-1921
30,000 (Publisher's statement paid)
C. Blythe Andrews Sr.
C. Blythe Andrews Jr.
letterpress
standard
Tuesday and Friday
1945
21
$3.00/col. inch (national & local)

West Palm Beach **Photo Illustrated News**
803 25th St. (33407)
   mailing address: P.O. Box 1583 (33402)
(305) 833-4071
4,000 (publisher's statement paid)
Mrs. M.A. Hall Williams
Mrs. M.A. Hall Williams
offset
tabloid
Thursday
1955
5
$2.66/col. inch national; $2.10/col. inch local

GEORGIA

Albany **Albany Times**
315 Highland Ave. (31705)
(912) 435-8700
3,000 (publisher's statement paid)
W.L. Russell
W.L. Russell
offset
standard
Thursday
1964
3
NA

Albany **Southwest Georgian**
310 S. Jackson (31701)
   mailing address: P.O Box 1941 (31701)
(912) 436-2156
10,000 (publisher's statement paid and free)
A.C. Searles
A.C. Searles
offset
standard
Friday
1940
6
$1.00/col. inch national; $.80/col. inch local

Atlanta **Atlanta Inquirer**
787 Parsons St. S.W. (30314)
   mailing address: P.O. Box 92367, Morris Brown Station (30314)
(404) 523-6086
32,000 (publisher's statement paid and free)
Jesse Hill Jr.
Ernest Pharr and D.L. Stanley
offset
standard
Thursday
1960
15
$2.93/col. inch (national)

Atlanta **Atlanta Voice**
1066 Washington St. S.W. (30315)
(404) 524-6426
35,000 (publisher's statement paid and free)
J. Lowell Ware
J. Lowell Ware and B. Norwood Chaney
offset
standard
Thursday
1966
8
$4.90/col. inch (national)

Augusta **News Review**
1030 Green Street (30902)
(404) 722-4555
5,600 (publisher's statement paid)
Mallory Millender
Mallory Millender
offset
standard
Thursday
1971
8
$2.35/col. inch (national)

Cordele **Southeastern News**
308 W. 16th Ave.
(912) 273-6714
Eugene Rutland

Columbus **Columbus Times**
1304 Midway Drive (31906)
   mailing address: P.O. Box 2845 (31901)
(404) 324-2404
10,000 (publisher's statement paid)
Mrs. Ophelia Mitchell
Mrs. Ophelia Mitchell
offset
standard
Wednesday
1958
14
$3.50/col. inch (national)

Macon **Macon Times**
589 Cotton Ave. (31201)
(912) 743-4310
NA
Willie L. Russell
Bob Scott
offset
standard
Thursday
1966
5
NA

Savannah **Savannah Herald**
808 Montgomery St. (31402)
   mailing address: P.O. Box 41 (31402)
(912) 232-4505
5,300 (publisher's statement paid and free)
Floyd Adams Sr.
Floyd Adams Jr.
offset
tabloid
Wednesday
1945
6
$1.50/col. inch (national)

Savannah **Tribune**
916 West Montgomery St. (31402)
(912) 233-6128
5,000 (publisher's statement paid)
Robert James
Angela Crawford
offset
standard
Wednesday
4
$2.75/col. inch (open rate)

ILLINOIS

Chicago **Bilalian News**
Cottage Grove Avenue
(312) 651-7600
150,000 (publisher's statement paid)
Nation of Islam
Ghayth Nur Kashif

Chicago **Chicago Metro News**
2600 S. Michigan Ave. (60616)
(312) 842-5950
NA
Charles B. Armstrong
Charles B. Armstrong
offset
standard
Thursday
1972
NA
NA

Chicago **Citizen**
412 E. 87th St. (60619)
(312) 487-7700
66,309 -- A group of three controlled circulation·
        newspapers including:
        Chatham and Southeast Citizen (26,630)
        Chicago Weekend (21,304)
        South End Citizen (18,375)
Augustus A Savage
Augustus A. Savage
offset
tabloid
Thursday
1965
7
$.90/line (national); $.80/line (local)
Ad rates include coverage in all 3 papers.

Chicago **Independent Bulletin**
728 W. 65th St. (60621)
(312) 783-1040
35,000 (controlled circulation)
Hurley Green Sr.
Hurley Green III
offset
tabloid
Friday
1958
7
NA

Chicago **New Crusader**
6429 S. Martin L. King Drive (60637)
(312) 752-2500
21,000 (controlled circulation)
Mrs. Dorothy R. Leavell
Joseph H. Jefferson
offset
tabloid
Thursday
1940
8
$.56/line national; $.30/line local

Chicago **Sentinel**
11740 South Elizabeth (60643)
(312) 568-7091
20,000 (publisher's statement paid and free)
Al Johnson·
Tony Miller
offset
tabloid
Thursday
1977
10
$.56/line national; $.45/line local

East St. Louis **Crusader**
2206 Missouri Ave. (62205)
(618) 271-2000
13,000 (publisher's statement paid and free)
Joe W. Lewis Sr.
Wesley McNeese
offset
standard
Thursday
1941
11
$.25/line (national)

East St. Louis **Monitor**
1501 State St. (62205)
(618) 271-0468
18,000 (publisher's statement paid)
Clyde C. Jordan
Clyde C. Jordan
offset
standard
Thursday
1962
22
$.20/line (national)

Gary **Info**
1953 Broadway (46407)
(219) 882-5591
9,000 (publisher's statement paid)
James T. Harris Jr.
Mrs. James T. Harris Jr.
offset
tabloid
Thursday
1961
6
$.70/line national; $.36/line local

Indianapolis **Indiana Herald**
723 N. West St. (46208)
(317) 634-8117
5,000 (publisher's statement paid)
O.L. Tandy
O.L. Tandy
offset
tabloid
Thursday
1959
7
$2.80/col. inch national and local

Indianapolis **Indianapolis Recorder**
2901 N. Tacoma Ave. (46218)
(317) 924-5143
14,000 (ABC)
Marcus C. Stewart Sr.
Marcus C. Stewart Sr.
offset
standard
Thursday
1895
24
NA

IOWA

Des Moines **New Iowa Bystander**
1016 Forest Ave. (50314)
(515) 277-8736
3,000 (publisher's statement paid)
Carl Williams
Carl Williams
offset
standard
Thursday
1894
5
$2.00/col. inch

KANSAS

Kansas City **Kansas City Globe**
5121 Parallel Pkwy.
(913) 596-1006
Marian Jordan

Kansas City **Kansas City Voice**
2727 North 13th St.
(913) 371-0303
Gladys Adams

KENTUCKY

Louisville **The American Baptist**
1715 Chestnut St. (40203)
(502) 587-8714
2,200 (publisher's statement paid)
Association of Kentucky Baptists
J.D. Bottoms
letterpress
standard
Thursday
1880
3
no advertising

Louisville **Louisville Defender**
1720 Dixie Highway (40210)
(502) 772-2591
7,500 (ABC)
Kenneth Stanley
Kenneth Stanley
offset
standard
Thursday
1933
16
$.43/line national; $.36/line local

LOUISIANA

Baton Rouge **Community Leader**
1210 North Blvd. (70802)
   mailing address: P.O. Box 53307 New Orleans (70153)
(504) 343-0544
41,400 -- A group of five regional papers (publisher's statement
       paid) including:
       Alexandria **Community Leader** (5,000)
       Baton Rouge **Community Leader** (17,600)
       Lafayette-Acadiana **Community Leader** (6,000)
       Lake Charles **Community Leader** (3,500)
       Monroe **Community Leader** (9,300)
Al Lankster
Al Lankster
offset
standard
Thursday
1952
18
$.50/line national; $.35/line local for ads
run in all 5 papers.

New Orleans **Louisiana Weekly**
640 S. Rampart St. (70113)
(504) 522-5696
17,000 (ABC)
C.C. Dejoie Jr.
C.C. Dejoie Jr.
offset
standard
Wednesday
1926
24
$.35/line (national)

Shreveport **Shreveport Sun**
1030 Texas Ave. (71166)
   mailing address: P.O. Box 1742 (71166)
(318) 425-1582 or 424-7125
18,500 (publisher's statement paid)
Shreveport Sun Inc.
Melvin L. Collins Jr.
offset
standard
Thursday
1920
7
$.20/line (national)

MARYLAND

Baltimore **Afro American**
628 N. Eutaw St. (21201)
   mailing address: P.O. Box 1857 (21203)
(301) 728-8200
27,000 (Tuesday); 25,000 (Friday) (ABC)
National Edition: 14,000 (Saturday)
John Murphy III
Ralph Matthews
letterpress
standard
Tuesday and Friday
1892
140
$1.10/line national; $.58/line local

MASSACHUSETTS

Boston **Bay State Banner**
25 Ruggles St. (Roxbury) (02119)
(617) 442-4900
10,000 (publisher's statement paid)
Melvin B. Miller
Melvin B. Miller
offset
tabloid
Thursday
1965
10
$.40/line (national & local)

MICHIGAN

Detroit **Michigan Chronicle**
479 Ledyard (48201)
(313) 963-5522
40,000 (ABC)
Longworth Quinn
Longworth Quinn
offset
standard
Wednesday
1936
36
NA

Ecorse **Ecorse Telegram**
4122 10th St. (48229)
(313) 928-2955
3,000 (publisher's statement paid)
J.C. Wall
J.C. Wall
offset
tabloid
Thursday
1945
4
NA
Flint **Spokesman**
3604 W. Saginaw St.
(313) 785-8751
5,000 (publisher's statement paid)
Thomas Terry
Mrs. DeRoney
offset
tabloid
Friday
NA
3
NA
Grand Rapids **Grand Rapids Times**
346 Wealthy St. S.E. (49503)
    mailing address: P.O. Box 2521
(616) 458-1279
12,000 (publisher's statement paid)
John Bankston
John Bankston
offset
tabloid
Wednesday
1957
2
$3.75/col. inch (national)
Jackson **Jackson Blazer**
1224 Francis St. (49203)
(517) 787-0450
6,000 (publisher's statement paid)
Ben Wade
Benita Wade
offset
tabloid
Monday
1962
3
$2.24/col. inch national; $2.10/col. inch local

Minneapolis **Minneapolis Spokesman and Recorder**
3744 4th Ave. S. (54409)
(612) 827-4021
13,000 (publisher's statement paid)
Mrs. Cecil E. Newman
Oscar Newman
offset
standard
Thursday
1934
6
$5.30/col. inch open rate

Minneapolis **Twin Cities Courier**
84 S. 6th St. Suite 501 (55402)
(612) 336-9618
15,000 (publisher's statement paid)
Mary J. Kyle
Mary J. Kyle
offset
standard
Thursday
1966
15
NA

St. Paul **St. Paul Recorder**
1015 Pioneer Building (55101)
(612) 222-0922
12,0000 (publisher's statement paid)
Mrs. Cecil Newman
Oscar Newman
letterpress
standard
Thursday
1934
same staff as **Minneapolis Spokesman**
see **Minneapolis Spokesman** for ad rate

MISSISSIPPI

Jackson **Jackson Advocate**
115 East Hamilton (39202)
(601) 948-2368
8,000 (combined paid and give away)
Charles W. Tinsdale
Dr. Zemu H. Akuchu
offset
standard
Thursday
1940
11
$6.30/col. inch national; $3.00/col. inch local

Meridan **Memo Digest**
2511 Fifth St. (39301)
   mailing address: P.O. Box 5782 (39301)
(601) 693-2372
5,000 (combined paid and give away)
Robert E. Williams
Robert E. Williams
offset
tabloid
Tuesday
1966
4
NA

MISSOURI

Kansas City **The Call**
1715 E. 18th St. (64108)
   mailing address: P.O. Box 477 (64141)
(816) 842-3804
13,462 (ABC)
Mrs. Ada C. Franklin
Miss Lucile Bluford
offset
standard
Friday
1919
25
$5.20/col. inch national; $4.20/col. inch local

St. Louis **St. Louis American**
3956 W. Florissant Ave. (63107)
(314) 531-0352
9,000 (publisher's statement paid)
Nathaniel Sweet
Bennie G. Rodgers
offset
standard
Thursday
1928
5
$.18/line (national); $.16/line (local)

St. Louis **St. Louis Argus**
4595 Martin Luther King Drive (63113)
(314) 531-1323
18,000 (publisher's statement paid)
Dr. Eugene Mitchell
Scot Anderson
offset
standard
Thursday
1912
20
$.50/line open rate

St. Louis **St. Louis Crusader**
4371 Finney Ave. (63113)
(314) 531-5860
8,000 (publisher's statement paid)
Henry Cockrell
Henry Cockrell
offset
standard
Monday
1963
4
NA

St. Louis **Evening World**
Riverview Blvd. (63113)
(314) 381-6990
3,400 (publisher's statement paid)
Benjamin Thomas
Benjamin Thomas
offset
tabloid
Monday
NA
1
$3.00/col. inch (national)

St. Louis **St. Louis Metro-Sentinel**
3338 Olive Ave., Suite 206 (33103)
(314) 531-2101
36,000 (paid and free publisher's statement)
Mrs. Howard B. Woods
NA
offset
standard
Thursday
1968
12
$.52/line national; $.47/line local

NEBRASKA

Omaha **Omaha Star**
2216 North 24th St. (68111)
30,000 (paid and free publisher's statement)
Mrs. Mildred Brown
Mrs. Mildred Brown
offset
standard
Thursday
1938
15
NA

NEVADA

N. Las Vegas **Las Vegas Voice**
North "H" St. (89106)
   mailing address: P.O. Box 4038 (89106)
(702) 648-2615
6,500 (publisher's statement paid)
Lawrence Albert
Lawrence Albert
offset
tabloid
Wednesday
1963
4
$2.50/col. inch (national & local)

NEW JERSEY

Newark **Afro-American**
11 Hill Street, Suite 200 (07102)
(201) 248-3636
6,000 (publisher's statement paid)
John Murphy
Robert C. Queen
letterpress
standard
Wednesday
1940
8
$.38/line national; $.32/line local

NEW YORK

Brooklyn **New York Recorder**
86 Bainbridge (11207)
   mailing address: P.O. Box D, East New York Station (11207)
(212) 493-4616
29,400 (publisher's statement paid)
Tom Bar Publishing Co.
Thomas Watkins Sr.
offset
tabloid
Thursday
1953
7
$.90/line national; $.80/line local

Buffalo **Buffalo Challenger**
1301 Filmore (14211)
(716) 897-0442 or 897-0715
35,000 (controlled circulation)
Arthur Eve
Mrs. Elaine Clark
offset
tabloid
Wednesday
1962
3
$.22/line (national); $2.45/col. inch (local)

Buffalo **Buffalo Criterion**
623-25 William (14206)
(716) 853-2973
NA
Frank E. Merriweather Jr.
Frank E. Merriweather Jr.
offset
standard
Wednesday
1925
5
NA
Buffalo **Fine Print**
1490 Jefferson St. (14204)
(716) 884-1490 or 852-3232
22,000 (publisher's statement paid and free)
Ronald H. Fleming
Ronald H. Fleming
offset
tabloid
Monday
1971
5
$.30/line (national); $.25/line (local)
Flushing **New York Voice**
78-36 Parson's Blvd. (11366)
(212) 657-6600
83,000 (publisher's statement paid)
Kenneth Drew
James Hicks
offset
tabloid
Thursday
1958
12
$1.60/line open rate
Hastings-on-Hudson **Westchester Country Press**
61 Pinecrest Drive (10706)
(914) 478-0006 or 478-3297
6,100 (publisher's statement paid)
Alger Adams
Alger Adams
offset
tabloid
Thursday
1910
8
$.14/line (national)

Mount Vernon **Westchester Observer**
542 E. Third St. (10553)
(914) 664-0052
10,000 (publisher's statement paid)
Ben Anderson
Ben Anderson
offset
tabloid
Thursday
1974
4
$3.00/col. inch open rate

New York **New York Amsterdam News**
2340 8th Ave. (10027)
(212) 678-6600
80,000 (ABC)
John Procope
Bryant Rollins
offset
tabloid
Thursday
1909
70
$1.25/line national; $1.00/line local

Rochester **Communicade**
Magnolia Ave.
   mailing address: P.O. Box 7933 (14606)
(716) 235-6695
2,500 (publisher's statement paid)
Ronald Cheatham
Ronald Cheatham
offset
tabloid
1972
5
$2.00/col. inch open rate

Syracuse **Gazette**
1313 South Salina St. (13205)
(315) 479-5587
15,000 (publisher's statement paid)
Willie Morgan
Kofi Quaye
offset
tabloid
1972
8
NA

Charlotte **Charlotte Post**
1524 West Blvd. (28208)
(704) 376-0496
9,103 (publisher's statement paid)
Bill Johnson
Bill Johnson
offset
standard
Thursday
1918
9
$.28/line national; $2.50/col. inch local

Charlotte **Star of Zion**
401 E. 2nd St. (28201)
    mailing address: P.O. Box 1047 (28201)
(704) 377-4329
7,600 (publisher's statement paid)
African Methodist Episcopal Zion Publishing House
Rev. M.B. Robinson
letterpress
tabloid
Thursday
1876
2
NA

Durham **Carolina Times**
436 E. Pettigrew St. (27701)
(919) 682-2913 or 688-6587
6,000 (publisher's statement paid)
Vivian Austin Edmonds
Lodius Austin
offset
standard
Thursday
1927
12
$.40/line (national)

Greensboro **Carolina Peacemaker**
Southeastern Bldg. Suite 530, Elm and Market Sts. (27401)
    mailing address: P.O. Box 20853 (27420)
(919) 274-6210
11,100 (publisher's statement paid)
Dr. John M. Kilimanjaro
Stan Davis
offset
standard
Thursday
1965
14
$.28/line (national); $2.40/col. inch (local)

Raleigh **Carolinian**
518 E. Martin St. (27601)
    mailing address: P.O. Box 25308 (27601)
(919) 834-5558
9,400 (publisher's statement paid)
P.R. Jervay Sr.
Charles R. Jones
offset
standard
Wednesday
1940
20
$.26/line national; $2.35/col. inch local

Wilmington **Wilmington Journal**
412 S. 7th St. (28401)
    mailing address: P.O. Box 1618 (28401)
(919) 762-5502
7,200 (publisher's statement paid)
Thomas Jervay Sr.
Thomas Jervay Sr.
offset
standard
Thursday
1945
6
$.20/line (national)

Winston-Salem **Chronicle**
102 West 4th Street (27102)
   mailing address: P.O. Box 3154 (27102)
(919) 723-9863
7,838 (publisher's statement paid)
Ernest Pitts
Ernest Pitts
offset
standard
Thursday
1974
9
$.40/line national; $2.75/col. inch local

OHIO

Akron **Reporter**
1134 S. Main St.
   mailing address: P.O. Box 2042 (44309)
(216) 253-0007
35,000 (publisher's statement paid)
Educator Publishing Co.
William Ellis
offset
tabloid
1969
NA
NA

Bedford Heights **Cleveland Metro**
22801 Aurora Road (44146)
(216) 663-5500
50,000 (controlled circulation)
William Rini
John Lenear
offset
standard
Monday
1955
3
$.21/line national

Cincinnati **Call and Post**
2940 Gilbert Ave. (45206)
(513) 751-2289
2,468 (ABC)
William O. Walker
to be named
offset
standard
Wednesday
1950
2
$.65/line national; $.32/line local

Cincinnati **Cincinnati Herald**
863 Lincoln Ave. (45206)
(513) 221-5440
12,000 (publisher's statement paid)
Miss Marjorie Parham
Ray Paul
offset
standard
Thursday
1956
7
$.35/line open rate

Cleveland **Call and Post**
1949 E. 105th St. (44106)
    mailing address: P.O. Box 6237 (44101)
(216) 791-7600
22,453 (ABC)
William O. Walker
William O. Walker
offset
standard
Wednesday
1920
50
$.65/line National; $.50/line local

Cleveland **South East Times**
3249 E. 137th Street (44120)
(216) 921-5337
20,000 (controlled circulation)
Michael Potts
Jim Baker
offset
tabloid
Friday
NA
5
$5.00/col. inch open rate

Columbus **Call and Post**
721 E. Long St. (43215)
(614) 224-8123
10,022 (ABC)
William O. Walker
Amos Lynch
offset
standard
Thursday
1960
12
$.65/line national; $.50/line local

Dayton **Jetstone News**
627 Salem Ave.
(513) 277-9307
24,000 (publisher's statement paid and free)
Harvey Simmons
Joan Shoup
offset
standard
Wednesday
1974
12
$6.00/col. inch open rate

Youngstown **Buckeye Review**
623 Belmont St. (44502)
   mailing address: P.O. Box 1436 (44501)
4,000 (publisher's statement paid)
Buckeye Review Publishing Co.
Mrs. Margaret Linton
offset
tabloid
Friday
1937
3
$2.00/col. inch open rate

OKLAHOMA

Lawton **Community Guide**
1929 McKinley Ave. (73501)
(405) 355-2424
5,000 (publisher's statement paid)
Robert K. Goodwin
Robert K. Goodwin
offset
Tabloid
Thursday
1971
12
$1.00/col. inch (national)

Oklahoma City **Black Dispatch**
1301 North Eastern (73104)
   mailing address: P.O. Box 1254 (73104)
(405) 424-4396
26,800 (publisher's statement paid and free)
John Dungee Sr.
Russell Perry
offset
standard
Thursday
1909
6
$2.10/col. inch (national)

Tulsa **Oklahoma Eagle**
122 N. Greenwood St. (74106)
(918) 582-7124
12,000 (publisher's statement paid)
E.L. Goodwin Sr.
Charles Jeffrey Jr.
offset
standard
Wednesday
1921
20
$2.00/col. inch (national)

OREGON

Portland Portland Observer
2201 N. Killingsworth (97217)
   mailing address: P.O. Box 3137 (97208)
(503) 283-2486
6,000 (publisher's statement paid)
Rev. Alfred Lee Henderson
Rev. Alfred Lee Henderson
offset
standard
Thursday
1970
4
$2.94/col. inch (national)

Portland Skanner
4845 N.E. Union Ave. (97211)
   mailing address: P.O. Box 11252 (97211)
(503) 287-3562
10,500 (publisher's statement paid and free)
Bernard V. Foster
Bernard V. Foster
offset
tabloid
Thursday
1975
6
$5.60/col. inch open rate

PENNSYLVANIA

Philadelphia Afro American
427 S. Broad St. (19147)
(215) 735-6160
4,300 (ABC)
John Murphy III
Mildred O'Neill
letterpress
standard
Monday
1935
4
$.25/line national and local

Philadelphia **New Observer**
1218 Chestnut St.
(215) 922-5220
15,000 (publisher's statement paid and free)
NA
J. Hugo Warren III
offset
tabloid
Thursday
1978
5
$.75/line open rate

Philadelphia **Philadelphia Tribune**
520-26 South 16th St. (19146)
(215) 546-1005
40,000-Tuesday; 60,000-Friday (ABC)
Philadelphia Tribune Corp.
Claude Harrison Jr.
offset
standard
Tuesday and Friday
1885
57
$9.80/col. inch national; $4.20/col. inch local

Pittsburgh **New Pittsburgh Courier**
315 E. Carson St. (15219)
(412) 481-8302
18,000 (ABC)
John H. Sengstacke
James D. Lewis
offset
standard
Thursday
1910
30
$.60/line open rate

Charleston **Charleston Chronicle**
534 King St. (29403)
   mailing address: P.O. Box 2548 (29403)
(803) 723-2785
3,5000 (publisher's statement paid)
J. John French
J. John French
offset
standard
Wednesday
1971
9
$3.00/col. inch local; $.28/line national

Columbia **Black News**
1310 Harden St. (29204)
   mailing address: P.O. Box 11128 (29211)
(803) 799-5252
23,000 (publisher's statement paid and free)
Brother Redfern II
Brother Redfern II
offset
standard
Wednesday
1973
7
$.700/col. inch national; $4.00/col. inch local

Memphis **Tri State Defender**
124 E. Calhoun (38101)
   mailing address: P.O. Box 2065 (38101)
(901) 526-8397
8,000 (ABC)
Robert Sengstacke
NA
offset
standard
Saturday
1951
15
$.35/line national and local

Nashville **Christian Recorder**
414 8th Ave. S. (37203)
(615) 255-1781
6,000 (publisher's statement paid and free)
African Methodist Episcopal Church
Rev. B.J. Nolen
letterpress
standard
Tuesday
1846
3
no advertising

TEXAS

Austin **Capital City Argus**
1704 East 12th (78702)
   mailing address: P.O. Box 6171 (78767)
(512) 476-0211
4,000 (publisher's statement paid and free)
Arthur Sims
Lois Sims
offset
tabloid
Thursday
1962
2
$1.50/col. inch (national and local)

Dallas **Dallas Weekly**
2700 Grand Ave. (75215)
(214) 428-8958
40,000 (controlled circulation)
Tony Davis
Tony Davis
offset
tabloid
Thursday
1953
7
$3.00/col. inch (national)

Dallas **Key News**
2241 Cedar Crest (75203)
(214) 946-1992
10,000 (publisher's statement paid and free)
Al Smith
Al Smith
offset
tabloid
Thursday
1960
5
NA

Dallas **Post Tribune**
3428 Sunnyvale (75216)
(214) 376-6400
16,000 (publisher's statement paid)
Post Tribune Corporation
Mrs. Dickie Foster
standard
Thursday
1949
5
$.25/line national; $2.25/col. inch local

Fort Worth **Fort Worth Mind**
805 Bryan St. (76104)
(817) 534-4061
15,000 (publisher's statement paid and give away)
C.R. Wise and R.L. Milton
C.R. Wise and R.L. Milton
letterpress
standard
Thursday
1932
3
$2.10/col. inch

Houston **Defender**
4406 Chartes St. (77004)
   mailing address: P.O. Box 8005 (77004)
(713) 529-3341
8,000 (controlled circulation)
C.F. Richardson Jr.
C.F. Richardson Jr.
offset
tabloid
Friday
1934
1
$.25/line (national)

Houston **Forward Times**
4411 Alemeda St. (77004)
(713) 526-4727
30,166 (ABC)
Mrs. Lenora Carter
Varee Shields
offset
tabloid
Wednesday
1960
42
$.35/line national; $.20/line local

Houston **Globe-Advocate**
3221 Southmore Blvd. (77004)
  mailing address: P.O. Box 8147 (77004)
(713) 524-1893
10,000 (controlled circulation)
E. Stanley Branch
R.A. Williams
offset
standard
Thursday
1965
6
$2.60/col. inch (national and local)

Houston **Houston Informer**
5703 Almeda St. (77004)
(713) 527-8261
10,000 (publisher's statement paid)
Pauline Watson
George McElroy
offset
standard
Tuesday
1892
11
$5.60/col. inch national; $3.92/col. inch local

Lubbock **West Texas Times**
Farm Road 1585 (79408)
    mailing address: P.O. Box 225 (79408)
(806) 763-4291
2,500 (publisher's statement paid)
Publication Service Co.
Thomas J. Patterson
offset
tabloid
Thursday
1962
3
$1.90/col. inch national: $1.50/col. inch local

San Antonio **San Antonio Register**
1501 E. Commerce (78203),
    mailing address: P.O. Box 1598 (78296)
(512) 222-1721
11,500 (publisher's statement paid)
Valmo C. Bellinger
U.J. Andrews
offset
standard
Thursday
1930
6
$.12/col. inch (national)

Waco **Waco Messenger**
504 Clifton St. (76704)
    mailing address: P.O. Box 2087 (76703)
(817) 799-6911
3,000 (publisher's statement paid)
M.P. Harvey
M.P. Harvey
letterpress
standard
Friday
1927
3
$2.00/col. inch (national)

Charlottesville **Albermarle Tribune**
1055 Grady Ave. (22903)
  mailing address: P.O. box 3428 (22902)
(703) 296-7058
3,300 (publisher's statement paid)
Randolph L. White
Randolph L. White
offset
standard
Thursday
1954
4
$.90/col. inch (national)

Norfolk **Journal and Guide**
1017 Church Street (23504)
(804) 625-3686
23,000 (publisher's statement paid)
Dr. Milton Reid
Miss Maravia Reid
offset
standard
Wednesday
1909
NA
$.80/line national; $.61/line local

Richmond **Afro-American**
301 E. Clay St. (23219)
(804) 649-8478
12,000 (ABC)
John H. Murphy III
Raymond H. Boone
letterpress
standard
Thursday
1939
12
$.52/line national; $.42/line local

Roanoke **Roanoke Tribune**
312 First St. N.W. (24016)
(703) 343-0326
4,000 (publisher's statement paid)
Claudia A. Whitworth
Claudia A. Whitworth
offset
tabloid
Thursday
1940
3
$1.40/col. inch

WASHINGTON

Seattle **Facts News**
2803 E. Cherry St. (98122)
(206) 324-0552
10,000 (publisher's statement paid and free)
Fitzgerald Beaver
Fitzgerald Beaver
offset
standard
Thursday
1961
8
$2.75/col. inch

Seattle **Medium**
1419 31st Ave. S. (98144)
    mailing address: P.O. Box 22047 (98122)
(206) 323-3070
15,000 (publisher's statement paid and free)
Chris Bennett
Chris Bennett
offset
tabloid
Thursday
1970
8
$3.50/col. inch (national)

Tacoma **Facts News**
1325 Kay St. (98405)
(206) 627-5597
5,000 (publisher's statement paid and free)
Fitzgerald Beaver
Fitzgerald Beaver
offset
tabloid
1969
3
$2.75/col. inch (national)

WISCONSIN

Milwaukee **Community Journal**
3612 N. Greenbay Ave. (53212)
(414) 265-5300
20,000 (publisher's statement-give away)
Mrs. Patricia Thomas
Michael Holt
offset
tabloid
Wednesday
1976
10
$.55/line national; $.35/line local

Milwaukee **Milwaukee Courier**
2431 W. Hopkins (53206)
(414) 445-2031
8,253 (ABC)
Jerrell W. Jones
Walter Jones
offset
standard
Thursday
1963
14
$.60/line national; $.45/line local

Milwaukee **Star**
2431 W. Hopkins (53206)
(414) 445-2031
25,000 (controlled circulation)
Jerrell Jones
Walter Jones
offset
tabloid
Tuesday
1976
same staff as **Milwaukee Courier**
$.46/line national; $.35/line local

Racine **Courier**
1436 State St. (53404)
(414) 637-6155
10,000 (controlled circulation)
Jerrel W. Jones
Walter Jones
offset
standard
Wednesday
1972
10
$.36/line national; $.20/line local

III. BI-WEEKLY BLACK NEWSPAPERS

FLORIDA

Tallahassee **Capital Outlook**
630 West Brevard St. (32302)
  mailing address: P.O. Box 212 (32302)
(904) 224-2746
10,000 (give away)
Steven Beasley
Steven Beasley
offset
tabloid
every other Wednesday
1977
6
NA

NEW YORK

Poughkeepsie **Mid Hudson Herald**
  contact: Victor Morris
  effort to contact this paper
  failed as all calls were
  received by an answering service.

OHIO

Dayton **Black Press**
(513) 278-6553
  contact: Mr. Bickerstaff

ILLINOIS

Evanston **North Shore Examiner**
Pitner Ave. (60202)
(312) 328-3238
20,000 (controlled circulation)
Randolph R. Tomlinson
Randolph R. Tomlinson
offset
tabloid
5th and 20th of each month
1968
6
$2.60/col. inch (national)

INDIANA

Gary **Gary American**
2254-56 Broadway (46402)
(219) 884-9415
1,500
Fred "Kid" Harris
Fred "kid" Harris
offset
tabloid
NA
1927
1
NA

TEXAS

Fort Worth **Fort Worth Como Monitor**
5529 Wellesley Ave. (76107)
    mailing address: P.O. Box 885 (76101)
(817) 737-4288
1,250 (publisher's statement paid)
William H. Wilburn Sr.
William H. Wilburn Sr.
letterpress
standard
Thursday (every other week)
1940
3
NA

IV. BLACK NEWSPAPERS NO LONGER PUBLISHING

ALABAMA

Anniston **Mirror**
Huntsville **Huntsville Mirror**
Huntsville **The Weekly News**
Huntsville **Walker County Mirror**
Montgomery **Alabama Tribune**
Selma **Selma Sun-Post**
Tuscaloosa **Courier**
Tuskegee **Tuskegee Progressive Times**
Tuskegee **Tuskegeean**
Tuskegee **Voice**

ALASKA

Anchorage **Alaska Spotlight**

ARKANSAS

Hot Springs **The Citizen Weekly**
Little Rock **Southern Mediator Journal**
Little Rock **State Weekly News**

ARIZONA

Phoenix **Arizona Tribune**

CALIFORNIA

Altadena **Pasadena Eagle**
Bakersfield **Bakersfield Observer**
Bakersfield **Metro-Star**
Inglewood **News Advertiser**
Los Angeles **Citizens Voice**
Los Angeles **Firestone Park News**
Los Angeles **Los Angeles News Press**
Los Angeles **Watts Star Review**
Los Angeles **The Record**
Menlo Park **Ravenswood Post**
Oakland **The Black Panther**
Pomona **Pomona Clarion**
San Diego **Lighthouse**
San Francisco **Independent**
San Francisco **Spokesman**
Santa Anna **Orange County Star Review**
Stockdon **San Joaquin Progressor**

COLORADO

Denver **Denver Blade**
Denver **Denver Chronicle**
Denver **Denver Star**

CONNECTICUT

Bridgeport **Harambee**
Hartford **Hartford Star**
New Haven **The Crow**
New Haven **New Haven Star**

DISTRICT OF COLUMBIA

Washington **National-Crusader**
Washington **Times-News**

FLORIDA

Daytona Beach **Bulletin-Advertiser**
Ft. Lauderdale **Spur**
Ft. Lauderdale **Tri-City News**
Ft. Meyers **Ebony Star**
Lakeland **Weekly Bulletin**
Pensacola **Pensacola Times**
Tampa **News-Reporter**

GEORGIA

Atlanta **Face the Nation**
Atlanta **People's Crusader**
Augusta **Augusta Mirror**
Augusta **Augusta Voice**
Augusta **Free Press**
Augusta **Weekly Review**
Columbus **News**
Macon **The Macon Weekly**
Thomasville **Thomasville-Tallahassee News**

ILLINOIS

Champaign **Illinois Times**
Chicago **Chicago Courier**
Chicago **Chicago Gazette**
Chicago **Woodlawn Observer**
Chicago **South Suburban News**
East St. Louis **Bi-State Defender**
East St. Louis **Defender**
East St. Louis **Empire Star Bulletin**
Joliet **Joliet Voice**
Rock Island **New Times**
Rockford **Rockford Crusader**
Springfield **Springfield Chronicle**

INDIANA

Gary **Gary Chronicle**
Gary **New Crusader**
South Bend **Reformer**

IOWA

Waterloo **Waterloo Defender**

KANSAS

Topeka **Ebony Times**
Topeka **Messenger**
Wichita **Enlightener**
Wichita **News Hawk**
Wichita **Wichita Times**

LOUISIANA

Baton Rouge **News Leader Group**
Bossier City **Hurricane**
Lafayette **Blaze**
New Orleans **Black Data Weekly**

MASSACHUSETTS

Boston **Boston Sun**
Boston **Hellenic Chronicle**
Boston **New Boston Citizen**
Boston **Boston News**
Boston **Roxbury News**
Springfield **Springfield Star**

MICHIGAN

Detroit **Courier**
Detroit **Michigan Scene**
Detroit **Tribune**
Kalamazoo **Kalamazoo Ledger**
Saginaw **The Valley Star**
Ypsilanti **Conveyor**

MINNESOTA

Minneapolis **Twin City Observer**
St. Paul **St. Paul Sun**

MISSISSIPPI

Greenville **Delta Leader**
Greenville **Negro Leader**
Jackson **Mississippi Enterprise**
Jackson **Mississippi Free Press**
Mound Bayou **News Digest**
Natchez **Natchez News Leader**
Vicksburg **Citizens' Appeal**

MISSOURI

Kansas City **Black Progress Shopper News**
St. Louis **New Crusader**
St. Louis **People's Guide**
St. Louis **St. Louis Chronicle**
St. Louis **St. Louis Defender**
St. Louis **St. Louis Mirror**

NEW JERSEY

Atlantic City **Atlantic City Crusader**
Newark **Grafrica News**
Plainfield **Voice**

NEW YORK

Albany **Urban Star Bulletin**
Buffalo **Empire Star**
Buffalo **Empire State Bulletin**
Corona **East Elmhurst News**
New York **New York Age**
New York **Manhattan Tribune**
New York City **New York Courier**

NORTH CAROLINA

Asheville **Southern News**
Asheville **Black Post**
Charlotte **Metrolinian News**
Charlotte **Queen City Gazette**
Gastonia **Gaston Times**
Greensboro **Future Outlook**

OHIO

Cincinnati **Black Dispatch**
Cincinnati **Cincinnati News**
Cleveland **Advocator**
Cleveland **It's Happening**
Columbus **Ohio Sentinel**
Columbus **Challenger**
Daytona **The Advocate**
Hamilton **Butler County American**
Toledo **Bronze Raven**
Youngstown **Mahoning Valley Challenger**

OKLAHOMA

Muskogee **Muskogee Herald**

OREGON

Portland **Northwest Clarion Defender**

PENNSYLVANIA

Philadelphia **Dig This Now**
Pittsburgh **Homewood-Brushton News**

RHODE ISLAND

Providence **North Star**

SOUTH CAROLINA

Anderson **Anderson Herald**
Camden **Camden Chronicle**
Columbia **Shopping Guide and News**
Kingstree **Carolina Sun**
Orangeburg **Black Voice**
Orangeburg **Orangeburg Herald**

TENNESSEE

Chattanooga **Chattanooga Observer**
Knoxville **Knoxville Times**
Memphis **Memphis Citizen**
Memphis **Memphis World**
Murfreesboro **Murfreesboro News**
Nashville **Capital City Defender**
Nashville **Independent Chronicle**
Nashville **Nashville Commentator**
Nashville **Union Review**

TEXAS

Austin **Inter-racial Review**
Dallas **Dallas Express**
Dallas **Elite News**
Dallas **Texas Times**
Fort Worth **Bronze Texan News**
Fort Worth **La Vida**
Houston **Houston Call**
Houston **Negro Labor News**
Houston **Tempo**
Houston **Voice of Hope**
San Antonio **New Generation**
San Antonio **Snap News**
Tyler **Tyler Leader**

VIRGINIA

Danville **Virginia News and Observer**
Petersburg **Digest and Reporter**

WASHINGTON

Seattle **Afro-American Journal**
Tacoma **Journal-Reporter**
Tacoma **Northwest Courier**

WEST VIRGINIA

Keystone **MacDowell Times**

WISCONSIN

Madison **Madison Sun**
Milwaukee **Greater Milwaukee Star**
Milwaukee **Milwaukee Star Times**
Milwaukee **Milwaukee Sun**
Milwaukee **Soul City Times**

Listed here are

seminal texts for those interested

Brooks, Maxwell R. **The Negro Press Re-Examined.**
Boston: Christopher Publishing Co., 1959.

Dann, Martin E. (ed.). **The Black Press 1827-1890.**
New York: G.P. Putnam and Sons, 1971.

Detweiler, Frederick D. **The Negro Press in the United States.**
Chicago: University of Chicago Press, 1922.

Fox, Stephen R. **The Guardian of Boston: William Monroe Trotter.**
New York: Atheneum, 1970.

Kerlin, Robert T. **The Voice of the Negro.**
New York: E.P. Dutton Co., 1920.

La Brie, Henry G. III. **The Black Press: A Bibliography.**
Kennebunkport, Maine: Mercer House Press, 1973.

Perspectives of the Black Press.
Kennebunkport, Maine: Mercer House Press, 1974.

A Survey of Black Newspapers in America.
Kennebunkport, Maine: Mercer House Press, 1979.

Murphy, Sharon. **Other Voices.**
Dayton: Pflaum, 1974.

Myrdal, Gunnar. **An American Dilemma.**
New York: Harper, 1944.

Oak, Vishnu. **The Negro Newpaper.**
Yellow Springs, Ohio: Antioch Press, 1948.

Ottley, Roi. **The Lonely Warrior.**
Chicago: Henry Regnery Co., 1955.

Penn, I Garland. **The Afro-American Press and Its Editors.**
Springfield, Mass.: Willey, 1981.

Sagarin, Mary. **John Brown Russwurm.**
New York: Lothrup, Lee and Shepard Co., 1970.

Thornbrough, Emma Lou. **T. Thomas Fortune: Millitant Journalist.**
Chicago: University of Chicago Press, 1972.

Ullman, Victor. **Martin R. Delany.**
Boston: Beacon Press, 1971.

Wolseley, Roland E. **The Black Press, U.S.A..**
Ames, Iowa: Iowa State University Press, 1971.